TWENTY POEMS OF ANNA AKHMATOVA

Anna Akhmatova

Translated From The Russian

by Jane Kenyon

with Vera Sandomirsky Dunham

Co–published by
NINETIES PRESS & ALLY PRESS
St. Paul ◆ Minnesota

Book design by Paul Feroe
No government funds were used to produce this book.

Library of Congress Cataloging-in-Publication Data

Akhmatova, Anna Andreevna, 1889-1966.
　　Twenty poems.

　　　Poems in English and Russian.
　　　Title on leaf preceding t.p.: Twenty poems of Anna
Akhmatova.
　　　1. Akmatova, Anna Andreevna, 1889-1966--Translations,
English.　I. Kenyon, Jane.　　II. Dunham, Vera Sandomirsky,
1912-　　　.　III. Title.　　IV. Title: 20 poems.
V. Title: Twenty poems of Anna Akhmatova.　VI. Title:
20 poems of Anna Akhmatova.
PG3476.A324A235　　1985　　　891.71'42　　　85-15769
ISBN 0-915408-30-9

First Printing, 1985; Third Printing, 1994
Co–published by Nineties Press and Ally Press

Distributed by **ALLY PRESS CENTER**, 524 Orleans St., St. Paul MN 55107
1-800-729-3002. Write or call for free catalog of books, tapes and videos.

For my mother
and in memory of my father

INTRODUCTION

As we remember Keats for the beauty and intensity of his shorter poems, especially the odes and sonnets, so we revere Akhmatova for her early lyrics—brief, perfectly-made verses of passion and feeling. Images build emotional pressure:

> And sweeter even than the singing of songs
> is this dream, now becoming real;
> the swaying of branches brushed aside,
> and the faint ringing of your spurs.

I love the sudden twists these poems take, often in the last line. In one poem the recollection of a literary party ends with the first frank exchange of glances between lovers. Another poem lists sweet-smelling things—minionette, violets, apples—and ends, astonishingly, "...we have found out forever/that blood smells only of blood." These poems celebrate the sensual life, and Akhmatova's devoted attention to details of sense always serves feeling:

> With the hissing of a snake the scythe cuts down
> the stalks, one pressed hard against another.

The snake's hissing is accurate to the sound of scythe mowing, and more than accurate: by using the snake for her auditory image, Akhmatova compares this rural place, where love has gone awry, to the lost Eden.

Akhmatova was born Anna Gorenko near Odessa in 1889. Soon her family moved to Tsarskoe Selo, near St. Petersburg, and there she began her education. Studying French, she learned to love Baudelaire and Verlaine. At the age of ten she became seriously ill, with a disease never diagnosed, and

1

went deaf for a brief time. As she recovered she wrote her first poems.

Money was not abundant in the Gorenko household, nor was tranquility. Akhmatova did not get on with her father, Andrei Gorenko, a naval engineer who lectured at the Naval Academy in St. Petersburg—also a notorious philanderer whose money went to his mistresses. (We know little of Akhmatova's relationship with her mother.) Akhmatova's brother Victor recalls an occasion when the young girl asked their father for money for a new coat. When he refused she threw off her clothes and became hysterical. (See *Akhmatova: Poems, Correspondence, Reminiscences, Iconography:* Ardis.) Andrei Gorenko deserted his family in 1905. A few years later, hearing that his daughter wrote verse, he asked her to choose a pen-name. He wished to avoid the ignominy, as he put it, of "a decadent poetess" in the family. She took her Tartar great-grandmother's name.

When Akhmatova was still a schoolgirl she met Nikolai Gumilev, a poet and founder of Acmeism who became her mentor and her first husband. Nadezhda Mandelstam has said that Akhmatova rarely spoke of her childhood; she seemed to consider her marriage to Gumilev the beginning of her life. (See Mandelstam's *Hope Abandoned:* Atheneum.) She was slow to accept his proposal. He sought her attention by repeated attempts at suicide until she finally married him in 1910. The bride's family did not attend the ceremony. Having won her at last, Gumilev promptly left to spend six months in Africa. On his return, while still at the train station, he asked her if she had been writing. By reply she handed him the manuscript of *Evening,* her first book.

Their son, Lev Gumilev, was born in 1912, the same year Akhmatova published *Evening.* By 1917, when she was twenty-eight, she had brought out two more books, *Rosary* and *White Flock.* Despite the historical tumult of World War I and the Revolution, her poetry quickly became popular. But tumult was private as well as public: by 1918 her mar-

2

riage had failed; Akhmatova divorced Gumilev and the same autumn married the Assyriologist V. K. Shileiko. This unhappy alliance—Shileiko burned his wife's poems in the samovar—lasted for six years. (See Amanda Haight's biography, *Akhmatova: A Poetic Pilgrimage*: Oxford.) Ordinary family life eluded Akhmatova, who went through many love affairs. Before her divorce from Shileiko, she lived in a ménage `a trois with Nikolai Punin and his wife; Punin later became her third husband. Motherhood was not easy. ("The lot of a mother is a bright torture: I was not worthy of it....") For the most part, Gumilev's mother raised her grandson Lev.

In the years following her early triumphs Akhmatova suffered many torments, as the Soviet regime hardened into tyranny. Gumilev was executed in 1921 for alleged anti-Bolshevik activity. Early in the twenties Soviet critics denounced Akhmatova's work as anachronistic and useless to the Revolution. The Central Committee of the Communist Party forbade publication of her verse; from 1923 to 1940, none of her poetry appeared in print. The great poems of her maturity, *Requiem,* and *Song Without a Hero,* exist in Russia today only by underground publication, or *samizdat.*

During the Stalinist terror of the 1930s the poet's son Lev and her husband Punin were imprisoned. Akhmatova's fellow Acmeist and close friend Osip Mandelstam died in a prison camp in 1938. (Punin died in another camp fifteen years later.) During the Second World War the Committee of the Communist Party of Leningrad evacuated Akhmatova to Tashkent in Uzbekistan. There she lived in a small, hot room, in ill-health, with Osip Mandelstam's widow Nadezhda.

In 1944 Akhmatova returned to Leningrad, to a still-higher wave of official antagonism. In a prominent literary magazine, Andrei Zhdanov denounced her as "...a frantic little fine lady flitting between the boudoir and the chapel...half-nun, half-harlot." The Union of Soviet Writers expelled her. A new book of poems, already in print, was seized and destroyed. For many years she supported herself only by working as a translator from Asiatic languages and from French, an activity she compared to "eating one's own brain" (Haight).

The final decade of her life was relatively tranquil. During the thaw that followed Stalin's death, the government released Lev Gumilev from labor camp and reinstated Akhmatova in the Writer's Union. She was permitted to publish and to travel. In Italy and England she received honors and saw old friends. She died in March, 1966, and was buried at Komarovo, near Leningrad.

Akhmatova's work ranges from the highly personal early lyrics through the longer, more public and political *Requiem*, on to the allusive and cryptic *Poem Without a Hero*. The early poems embody Acmeist principles. Acmeism grew out of the Poet's Guild, which Nikolai Gumilev and Sergei Gorodetsky founded in 1912—fifteen poets who met regularly to read poems and argue aesthetic theory. At one meeting, Gumilev proposed an attack on Symbolism with its "obligatory mysticism." He proposed Acmeism as an alternative; Acmeism held that a rose is beautiful in itself, not because it stands for something. These poets announced that they were craftsmen not priests, and dedicated themselves to clarity, concision, and perfection of form. They summed up their goals in two words: "beautiful clarity." Gumilev himself, Akhmatova and Osip Mandelstam were the leading Acmeists, and the movement thrived for a decade.

Written so many years later, *Requiem* and *Poem Without a Hero* naturally moved past Akhmatova's early poems in intention and in scope. They are manifestly political and historical. *Requiem* records the terror of the purges in the 1930s, commemorating the women who stood waiting outside prison gates with parcels for husbands, sons, and brothers; Akhmatova compares the suffering of these women to Mary's at the Crucifixion. In the prefatory note to *Poem Without a Hero* Akhmatova says: "I dedicate this poem to its first listeners—my friends and countrymen who perished in Leningrad during the siege."

These translations are free-verse versions of rhymed and metered poems. Losing the formal perfection of the Russian verses—much of their "beautiful clarity"—has been a constant source of frustration and sadness to me and to my co-worker, Vera Sandomirsky Dunham. But something, I think, crosses the barrier between our languages. Because it is impossible to translate with fidelity to form *and* to image, I have sacrificed form for image. Image embodies feeling, and this embodiment is perhaps the greatest treasure of lyric poetry. In translating, I mean to place the integrity of the image over all other considerations.

Translation provides many frustrations. It seems impossible to translate a single Russian syllable which means "What did he have to do that for?" Trying to translate lines about a native place—so important to Akhmatova, who firmly refused expatriation—how does one render *rodnoi*, which means "all that is dear to me, familiar, my own..."? I remember Vera clapping her hands to her head and moaning, "This will sink us..."

There are times when—in the interest of cadence, tone, or clarity—I have altered punctuation or moved something from one line to another. Often I needed to shift the verb from the end to the beginning of the sentence. Sometimes a word, translated from Russian as the dictionary would have it, made impossible English. I list significant variations from the original in notes at the back of this book. We have translated from the two volume *Works*, edited by G. P. Struve and B. A. Filippov, published by Interlanguage Literary Associates in 1965.

I want to thank Robert Bly, who first encouraged me to read Akhmatova, and later to translate these poems. I also thank Lou Teel, who, as a student of Russian at Dartmouth, helped me begin the work. I owe special thanks to Vera Sandomirsky Dunham, a busy scholar, teacher, and life-long lover of these poems. Her fear that a free-verse translation of Akhmatova is fundamentally misconceived has not prevented her from offering her time, her erudition, and her hospitality.

J.K.

Poems From
Evening (1912)
Rosary (1914)
White Flock (1917)

1

Память о солнце в сердце слабеет.
Желтей трава.
Ветер снежинками ранними веет
Едва-едва.

В узких каналах уже не струится —
Стынет вода.
Здесь никогда ничего не случится, —
О, никогда!

Ива на небе пустом распластала
Веер сквозной.
Может быть, лучше, что я не стала
Вашей женой.

Память о солнце в сердце слабеет.
Что это? Тьма?
Может быть!.. За ночь прийти успеет
Зима.

1911

The memory of sun weakens in my heart,
grass turns yellow,
wind blows the early flakes of snow
lightly, lightly.

Already the narrow canals have stopped flowing;
water freezes.
Nothing will ever happen here--
not ever!

Against the empty sky the willow opens
a transparent fan.
Maybe it's a good thing I'm not
your wife.

The memory of sun weakens in my heart.
What's this? Darkness?
It's possible. And this may be the first night
of winter.

1911

2

Вечерние часы перед столом.
Непоправимо белая страница.
Мимоза пахнет Ниццей и теплом.
В луче луны летит большая птица.

И, туго косы на ночь заплетя,
Как будто завтра нужны будут косы,
В окно гляжу я, больше не грустя,
На море, на песчаные откосы.

Какую власть имеет человек,
Который даже нежности не просит!
Я не могу поднять усталых век,
Когда мое он имя произносит.

1913

Evening hours at the desk.
And a page irreparably white.
The mimosa calls up the heat of Nice,
a large bird flies in a beam of moonlight.

And having braided my hair carefully for the night
as if tomorrow braids will be necessary,
I look out the window, no longer sad, --
at the sea, the sandy slopes.

What power a man has
who doesn't ask for tenderness!
I cannot lift my tired eyes
when he speaks my name.

1913

3

Знаю, знаю — снова лыжи
Сухо заскрипят.
В синем небе месяц рыжий,
Луг так сладостно покат.

Во дворце горят окошки,
Тишиной удалены.
Ни тропинки, ни дорожки,
Только проруби темны.

Ива, дерево русалок,
Не мешай мне на пути!
В снежных ветках черных галок,
Черных галок приюти.

1913

I know, I know the skis
will begin again their dry creaking.
In the dark blue sky the moon is red,
and the meadow slopes so sweetly.

The windows of the palace burn
remote and still.
No path, no lane,
only the iceholes are dark.

Willow, tree of nymphs,
don't get in my way.
Shelter the black grackles, black
grackles among your snowy branches.

1913

4

ГОСТЬ

Все как раньше: в окна столовой
Бьется мелкий метельный снег,
И сама я не стала новой,
А ко мне приходил человек.

Я спросила: „Чего ты хочешь?”
Он сказал: „Быть с тобой в аду”.
Я смеялась: „Ах, напророчишь
Нам обоим, пожалуй, беду”.

Но, поднявши руку сухую,
Он слегка потрогал цветы:
„Расскажи, как тебя целуют,
Расскажи, как целуешь ты”.

И глаза, глядевшие тускло,
Не сводил с моего кольца.
Ни один не двинулся мускул
Просветленно-злого лица.

О, я знаю: его отрада —
Напряженно и страстно знать,
Что ему ничего не надо,
Что мне не в чем ему отказать.

1 января 1914

The Guest

Everything's just as it was: fine hard snow
beats against the dining room windows,
and I myself have not changed:
even so, a man came to call.

I asked him: "What do you want?"
He said, "To be with you in hell."
I laughed: "It seems you see
plenty of trouble ahead for us both."

But lifting his dry hand
he lightly touched the flowers.
"Tell me how they kiss you,
tell me how you kiss."

And his half-closed eyes
remained on my ring.
Not even the smallest muscle moved
in his serenely angry face.

Oh, I know it fills him with joy--
this hard and passionate certainty
that there is nothing he needs,
and nothing I can keep from him.

1 January 1914

5

Н. В. Н.

Есть в близости людей заветная черта,
Ее не перейти влюбленности и страсти, —
Пусть в жуткой тишине сливаются уста
И сердце рвется от любви на части.

И дружба здесь бессильна, и гора
Высокого и огненного счастья,
Когда душа свободна и чужда
Медлительной истоме сладострастья.

Стремящиеся к ней безумны, а ее
Достигшие — поражены тоскою...
Теперь ты понял, отчего мое
Не бьется сердце под твоей рукою.

1915

N.V.N.

There is a sacred, secret line in loving
which attraction and even passion cannot cross,--
even if lips draw near in awful silence
and love tears at the heart.

Friendship is weak and useless here,
and years of happiness, exalted and full of fire,
because the soul is free and does not know
the slow luxuries of sensual life.

Those who try to come near it are insane
and those who reach it are shaken by grief.
So now you know exactly why
my heart beats no faster under your hand.

1915

6

Как белый камень в глубине колодца,
Лежит во мне одно воспоминанье.
Я не могу и не хочу бороться:
Оно — веселье и оно — страданье.

Мне кажется, что тот, кто близко взглянет
В мои глаза, его увидит сразу.
Печальней и задумчивее станет
Внимающего скорбному рассказу.

Я ведаю, что боги превращали
Людей в предметы, не убив сознанья.
Чтоб вечно жили дивные печали,
Ты превращен в мое воспоминанье.

1916
Слепнево

Like a white stone in a deep well
one memory lies inside me.
I cannot and will not fight against it:
it is joy and it is pain.

It seems to me that anyone who looks
into my eyes will notice it immediately,
becoming sadder and more pensive
than someone listening to a melancholy tale.

I remember how the gods turned people
into things, not killing their consciousness.
And now, to keep these glorious sorrows alive,
you have turned into my memory of you.

1916
Slepnevo

7

Все обещало мне его:
Край неба, тусклый и червонный,
И милый сон под Рождество,
И Пасхи ветер многозвонный,

И прутья красные лозы,
И парковые водопады,
И две большие стрекозы
На ржавом чугуне ограды.

И я не верить не могла,
Что будет дружен он со мною,
Когда по горным склонам шла
Горячей каменной тропою.

1916

Everything promised him to me:
the fading amber edge of the sky,
and the sweet dreams of Christmas,
and the wind at Easter, loud with bells,

and the red shoots of the grapevine,
and waterfalls in the park,
and two large dragonflies
on the rusty iron fencepost.

And I could only believe
that he would be mine
as I walked along the high slopes,
the path of burning stones.

1916

Poems From
Plantain (1921)

8

Да, я любила их, те сборища ночные, —
На маленьком столе стаканы ледяные,
Над черным кофеем пахучий, тонкий пар,
Камина красного тяжелый, зимний жар,
Веселость едкую литературной шутки
И друга первый взгляд, беспомощный и жуткий.

1917

Yes I loved them, those gatherings late at night,--
the small table, glasses with frosted sides,
fragrant vapor rising from black coffee,
the fireplace, red with powerful winter heat,
the biting gaiety of a literary joke,
and the first helpless and frightening glance of my love.

1917

9

Двадцать первое. Ночь. Понедельник.
Очертанья столицы во мгле.
Сочинил же какой-то бездельник,
Что бывает любовь на земле.

И от лености или со скуки
Все поверили, так и живут:
Ждут свиданий, боятся разлуки
И любовные песни поют.

Но иным открывается тайна,
И почиет на них тишина...
Я на это наткнулась случайно
И с тех пор все как будто больна.

1917

Twenty-first. Night. Monday.
Silhouette of the capitol in darkness.
Some good-for-nothing--who knows why--
made up the tale that love exists on earth.

People believe it, maybe from laziness
or boredom, and live accordingly:
they wait eagerly for meetings, fear parting,
and when they sing, they sing about love.

But the secret reveals itself to some,
and on them silence settles down . . .
I found this out by accident
and now it seems I'm sick all the time.

1917

10

В каждых сутках есть такой
Смутный и тревожный час.
Громко говорю с тоской,
Не раскрывши сонных глаз.
И она стучит, как кровь,
Как дыхание тепла,
Как счастливая любовь,
Рассудительна и зла.

1917

There is a certain hour every day
so troubled and heavy . . .
I speak to melancholy in a loud voice
not bothering to open my sleepy eyes.
And it pulses like blood,
is warm like a sigh,
like happy love
is smart and nasty.

1917

11

По твердому гребню сугроба
В твой белый, таинственный дом
Такие притихшие оба
В молчании нежном идем.
И слаще всех песен пропетых
Мне этот исполненный сон,
Качание веток задетых
И шпор твоих легонький звон.

Январь 1917

We walk along the hard crest of the snowdrift
toward my white, mysterious house,
both of us so quiet,
keeping the silence as we go along.
And sweeter even than the singing of songs
is this dream, now becoming real:
the swaying of branches brushed aside
and the faint ringing of your spurs.

January 1917

12

И целый день, своих пугаясь стонов,
В тоске смертельной мечется толпа,
А за рекой на траурных знаменах
Зловещие смеются черепа.
Вот для чего я пела и мечтала,
Мне сердце разорвали пополам,
Как после залпа сразу тихо стало,
Смерть выслала дозорных по дворам.

1917

All day the crowd rushes one way, then another;
its own gasping frightens it still more,
and laughing skulls fly on funereal banners,
prophesying from the river's far side.
For this I sang and dreamed!
They have torn my heart in two.
How quiet it is after the volley!
Death sends patrols into every courtyard.

1917

13

Течет река неспешно по долине,
Многооконный на пригорке дом.
А мы живем как при Екатерине:
Молебны служим, урожая ждем.
Перенеся двухдневную разлуку,
К нам едет гость вдоль нивы золотой,
Целует бабушке в гостиной руку
И губы мне на лестнице крутой.

Лето 1917

The river flows without hurry through the valley,
a house with many windows rises on the hill--
and we live as people did under Catherine;
hold church services at home, wait for harvest.
Two days have passed, two days' separation;
a guest comes riding along a golden wheatfield.
In the parlor he kisses my grandmother's hand,
and on the steep staircase he kisses my lips.

Summer 1917

14

Еще весна таинственная млела,
Блуждал прозрачный ветер по горам,
И озеро глубокое синело —
Крестителя нерукотворный храм.

Ты был испуган нашей первой встречей,
А я уже молилась о второй,
И вот сегодня снова жаркий вечер, —
Как низко солнце стало над горой...

Ты не со мной, но это не разлука:
Мне каждый миг — торжественная весть.
Я знаю, что в тебе такая мука,
Что ты не можешь слова произнесть.

Весна 1917

The mysterious spring still lay under a spell,
the transparent wind stalked over the mountains,
and the deep lake kept on being blue,--
a temple of the Baptist not made by hands.

You were frightened by our first meeting,
but I already prayed for the second, and now
the evening is hot, the way it was then . . .
How close the sun has come to the mountain.

You are not with me, but this is no separation:
to me each instant is--triumphant news.
I know there is such anguish in you
that you cannot say a single word.

Spring 1917

15

Я слышу иволги всегда печальный голос
И лета пышного приветствую ущерб,
А к колосу прижатый тесно колос
С змеиным свистом срезывает серп.

И стройных жниц короткие подолы,
Как флаги в праздник, по ветру летят.
Теперь бы звон бубенчиков веселых,
Сквозь пыльные ресницы долгий взгляд.

Не ласки жду я, не любовной лести
В предчувствии неотвратимой тьмы,
Но приходи взглянуть на рай, где вместе
Блаженны и невинны были мы.

1917

I hear the always-sad voice of the oriole
and I salute the passing of delectable summer.
With the hissing of a snake the scythe cuts down
the stalks, one pressed hard against another.

And the hitched-up skirts of the slender reapers
fly in the wind like holiday flags. Now if only
we had the cheerful ring of harness bells,
a lingering glance through dusty eyelashes.

I don't expect caresses or flattering love-talk,
I sense unavoidable darkness coming near,
but come and see the Paradise where together,
blissful and innocent, we once lived.

1917

16

Ты — отступник: за остров зеленый
Отдал, отдал родную страну,
Наши песни и наши иконы
И над озером тихим сосну.

Для чего ты, лихой ярославец,
Коль еще не лишился ума,
Загляделся на рыжих красавиц
И на пышные эти дома?

Так теперь и кощунствуй, и чванься,
Православную душу губи,
В королевской столице останься
И свободу свою полюби.

Для чего ж ты приходишь и стонешь
Под высоким окошком моим?
Знаешь сам, ты и в море не тонешь,
И в смертельном бою невредим.

Да, не страшны ни море, ни битвы
Тем, кто сам потерял благодать.
Оттого-то во время молитвы
Попросил ты тебя поминать.

1917
Слепнево

You are an apostate: for a green island
you give away your native land,
our songs and our icons
and the pine tree over the quiet lake.

Why is it, you dashing man from Yaroslav,
if you still háve your wits
why are you gaping at the beautiful red-heads
and the luxurious houses?

You might as well be sacrilegious and swagger,
finish off your orthodox soul,
stay where you are in the royal capital
and begin to love your freedom in earnest.

How does it happen that you come to moan
under my small high window?
You know yourself that waves won't drown you
and mortal combat leaves you without a scratch.

It's true that neither the sea nor battles
frighten those who have renounced paradise.
That's why at the hour of prayer
you asked to be remembered.

1917
Slepnevo

Various Later Poems

17

Привольем пахнет дикий мед,
Пыль — солнечным лучом,
Фиалкою — девичий рот,
А золото — ничем.

Водою пахнет резеда
И яблоком — любовь.
Но мы узнали навсегда,
Что кровью пахнет только кровь.

Wild honey has the scent of freedom,
dust--of a ray of sun,
a girl's mouth--of a violet,
and gold--has no perfume.

Watery--the minionette,
and like an apple--love,
but we have found out forever
that blood smells only of blood.

18

Не лирою влюбленного
Иду прельщать народ,
Трещотка прокаженного
В моих руках поет.

It is not with the lyre of someone in love
that I go seducing people.
The rattle of the leper
is what sings in my hands.

19

СКАЗКА О ЧЕРНОМ КОЛЬЦЕ

1

Мне от бабушки-татарки
Были редкостью подарки;
И зачем я крещена,
Горько гневалась она.
А пред смертью подобрела
И впервые пожалела
И вздохнула: „Ах, года!
Вот и внучка молода”.
И, простивши нрав мой вздорный,
Завещала перстень черный.
Так сказала: „Он по ней,
С ним ей будет веселей”.

2

Я друзьям моим сказала:
„Горя много, счастья мало”,
И ушла, закрыв лицо;
Потеряла я кольцо.
И друзья мои сказали:
„Мы кольцо везде искали,
Возле моря на песке
И меж сосен на лужке”.
И, догнав меня в аллее,
Тот, кто был других смелее,
Уговаривал меня
Подождать до склона дня.

Tale of the Black Ring

1

Presents were rare things
coming from my grandmother, a Tartar;
and she was bitterly angry
when I was baptized.
But she turned kind before she died
and for the first time pitied me,
sighing: "Oh the years!
and here my young granddaughter!"
Forgiving my peculiar ways
she left her black ring to me.
She said: "It becomes her,
with this things will be better for her."

2

I said to my friends:
"There is plenty of grief, so little joy."
And I left, covering my face;
I lost the ring.
My friends said:
"We looked everywhere for the ring,
on the sandy shore,
and among pines near the small clearing."
One more daring than the rest
caught up with me on the tree-lined drive
and tried to convince me
to wait for the close of day.

Я совету удивилась
И на друга рассердилась,
Что глаза его нежны:
„И на что вы мне нужны?
Только можете смеяться,
Друг пред другом похваляться
Да цветы сюда носить".
Всем велела уходить.

3

И, придя в свою светлицу,
Застонала хищной птицей,
Повалилась на кровать
Сотый раз припоминать:
Как за ужином сидела,
В очи темные глядела,
Как не ела, не пила
У дубового стола,
Как под скатертью узорной
Протянула перстень черный,
Как взглянул в мое лицо,
Встал и вышел на крыльцо.

. . . .

Не придут ко мне с находкой!
Далеко над быстрой лодкой
Заалели небеса,
Забелели паруса.

1917—1936

The advice astonished me
and I grew angry with my friend
because his eyes were full of sympathy:
"And what do I need you for?
You can only laugh,
boast in front of the others
and bring flowers."
I told them all to go away.

3

Coming into my cheerful room
I called out like a bird of prey,
fell back on the bed
to remember for the hundredth time
how I sat at supper
and looked into dark eyes,
ate nothing, drank nothing
at the oak table,
how under the regular pattern of the tablecloth
I held out the black ring,
how he looked into my face,
stood up and stepped out onto the porch.
. . . .
They won't come to me with what they have found!
Far over the swiftly moving boat
the sails turned white,
the sky flushed pink.

1917-1936

20

В ПУТИ

Земля хотя и не родная,
Но памятная навсегда,
И в море нежно-ледяная
И несоленая вода.

На дне песок белее мела,
А воздух пьяный, как вино,
И сосен розовое тело
В закатный час обнажено.

А сам закат в волнах эфира
Такой, что мне не разобрать,
Конец ли дня, конец ли мира,
Иль тайна тайн во мне опять.

1964

On the Road

Though this land is not my own
I will never forget it,
or the waters of its ocean,
fresh and delicately icy.

Sand on the bottom is whiter than chalk,
and the air drunk, like wine.
Late sun lays bare
the rosy limbs of the pine trees.

And the sun goes down in waves of ether
in such a way that I can't tell
if the day is ending, or the world,
or if the secret of secrets is within me again.

1964

NOTES

"The memory of sun weakens in my heart"...from *Evening*.

Line 15: Literally, "Maybe! This night will manage to come/winter."

"Evening hours at the desk"... from *Rosary*.

Line 3: Literally, "The mimosa smells of Nice and warmth."

"I know, I know the skis"...from *Rosary*.

Line 6: Literally, "removed by silence."

Line 8: Holes in the ice made by fishermen...

"The Guest"...from *Rosary*.

Line 13: Literally, "And his eyes gazing dimly..."

Lines 17 and 18: Literally, "Oh I know his bliss is to know (with stress, by force) and passionately..."

"There is a sacred, secret line"...from *White Flock*.

Line 1: Literally, "...in inloveness"..."being in love."

Line 3: Literally, "...even if lips blend..."

Line 5: Literally, "...friendship is impotent..."

Line 8: Literally, "...the slow langor of carnal passion."

"Like a white stone in a deep well"...from *White Flock*.

"Everything promised him to me..."from *White Flock*.

Line 10: Literally, "...that he would be friends with me."

Line 12: Literally, "...along the hot, stony path."

"Twenty-first. Night. Monday..." from *Plantain*.

Line 3: "...who knows why"—literally, "...what did he have to do that for?"

Line 8: Literally, "...they sing love songs."

"There is a certain hour every day"...from *Plantain*.

Line 3: Here translated as melancholy; in the Russian, *toska*: melancholy, yearning, boredom, sweet sadness, all at once. What is more, *toska* has a feminine gender. So *she* pulses like blood, *she's* warm like a sigh, etc., thereby making "sisters" of the speaker and the melancholy to which she addresses herself.

"We walk along the hard crest..." from *Plantain*.

In Russian the verb "walk" is delayed until line 4, and is coupled with an adjective meaning "soft" or "tender."

Line 8: Literally, "... the tinkling of your spurs."

"All day the crowd rushes..." from *Plantain*.

Lines 1 and 2: Literally, "And the whole day, turning frightened of its own gasps, in deadly agitation the crowd rushes."

"The mysterious spring..." from *Plantain*.

Line 8: Literally, "...how low the sun stands over the mountain."

"You are an apostate..." from *Plantain*.

Line 17: Literally, "Yes, neither the sea nor battles..."

"Wild honey has the scent of freedom..." from Struve, Vol. 2, p. 137. Poems of Various Years.

Line 4: Literally, "...and gold—of nothing."

Lines 5 and 6: Literally, "Of water smells the minionette,/and of apple—love." It seemed important to keep the abstractions—freedom and love—in parallel positions within their stanzas. I couldn't bring myself to say "Of water smells the minionette..."—that's not English. So I left out the verb and invented "watery."

"It is not with the lyre of someone in love..." from Struve, Vol. 2, p. 139.

"Tale of the Black Ring..."from Struve, Vol. 1, p. 180.

For Akhamatova the gift of the ring was synonymous with the gift of song.

Line 3: Grandmother was Muslim and baptism was foreign to her belief.

Line 27: Literally, ..."his eyes are tender."

"On the Road" from *Odd Number: Verses 1907-1964* (Struve, Vol. 1, p. 336.)

Lines 7 and 8: Literally, "and the pink body of pines/is naked in the sunset hour."

Jane Kenyon's first book of poetry, *From Room to Room*, was published by Alice James Books in 1978. She has been widely published in magazines including: *The New Republic, APR, Poetry, The Iowa Review,* and *The New Yorker.* In 1982 she was the recipient of a Fellowship Grant from the National Endowment for the Arts. She lives in Danbury, New Hampshire.

Vera Sandomirsky Dunham was born in Russia, came to the United States in 1940, and now lives on Long Island. She is a scholar and critic of Russian literature and has taught at several universities, including Columbia, where she is an Associate of the Harriman Institute. As a sociologist of literature she is known for her book *In Stalin's Time: Middleclass Values in Soviet Fiction,* Cambridge University Press, 1976 and 1979. She has worked with several American poets—Robert Bly, Louis Simpson, William Jay Smith—translating contemporary Russian poetry.